Rivers and Lakes

Lake Victoria

Cari Meister

ABDO Publishing Company

visit us at
www.abdopub.com

Published by ABDO Publishing Company, 4940 Viking Drive, Edina, Minnesota 55435.
Copyright © 2002 by Abdo Consulting Group, Inc. International copyrights reserved in all countries. No part of this book may be reproduced in any form without written permission from the publisher.

Printed in the United States.

Photo credits: Corbis

Contributing editors: Bob Italia, Tamara L. Britton, Kate A. Furlong, Kristin Van Cleaf
Book design and graphics: Neil Klinepier

Library of Congress Cataloging-in-Publication Data

Meister, Cari.
    Lake Victoria / Cari Meister.
        p. cm. -- (Rivers and lakes)
    Includes bibliographical references and index.
    Summary: Surveys the origin, geological borders, climate, water, plant and animal life, and economic and ecological aspects of the world's second largest lake.
    ISBN 1-57765-105-7 (alk. paper)
    1. Victoria, Lake--Juvenile literature. [1. Victoria, Lake.]
I. Title. II. Series.
GB1761.M45098
551.48'2'0967827--DC21

                                    98-7298
                                       CIP
                                        AC

Contents

Lake Victoria

*L*ake Victoria is a shallow, tropical lake in east-central Africa. It is the world's second-largest freshwater lake. North America's Lake Superior is the only freshwater lake larger than Lake Victoria.

Lake Victoria lies on a **plateau** between the Western and Eastern Rift Valleys. Most of the lake lies south of the **equator**. To the northwest, Lake Victoria is bordered by Uganda. Kenya is to the northeast, and Tanzania is to the south.

Lake Victoria supports many people, plants, and animals. But many of the lake's plant and animal species are **endangered**. Pollution and other factors have killed much of this wildlife. Today, scientists are studying ways to save the lake.

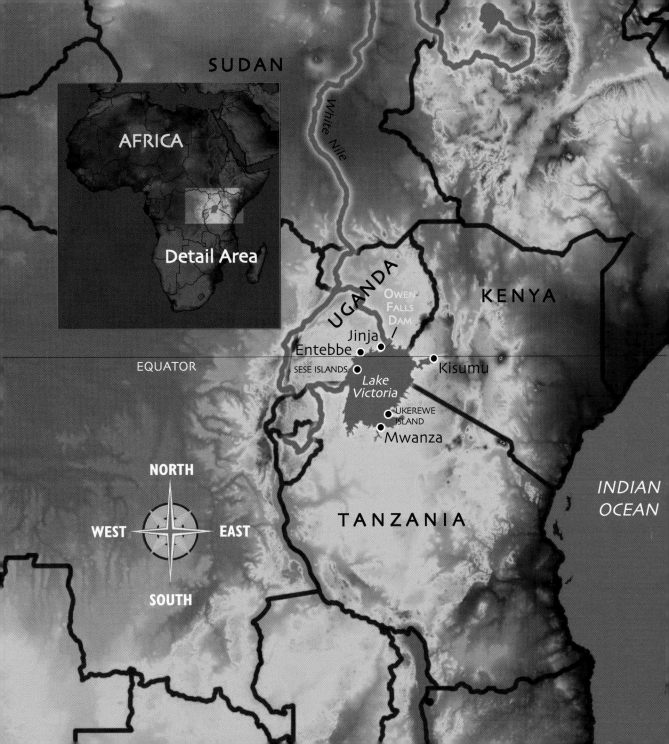

History

*P*eople have lived on the shores of Lake Victoria for hundreds of years. The Bantu people settled on the lake's shores around the 500s B.C. Later, around the A.D. 1500s, the Luo settled on the lake. They called it Ukerewe.

In 1858, British explorer John Speke explored the Nile River. He sailed south, into Ukerewe. He renamed it Lake Victoria, in honor of England's Queen Victoria.

Speke determined that Lake Victoria was the source of the White Nile. The White Nile is a **tributary** of the Nile River. The White Nile is the only outlet for Lake Victoria. It leaves the lake near Jinja, Uganda.

In 1954, Ugandans built a dam on the White Nile at Owen Falls. The dam caused Lake Victoria's water level to rise. The lake became a **reservoir** for the Nile River. Today, the Owen Falls Dam supplies electricity for people in Uganda and Kenya.

John Speke

Shores & Islands

*L*ake Victoria's shoreline has a varied landscape. The southwestern coast has cliffs 300 feet (91 m) high. There are papyrus and ambatch swamps on the western coast. The northern coast is flat and bare. Thousands of years of **erosion** have created many bays, gulfs, and river **inlets** there.

Lake Victoria has many islands. They vary in size from miles wide to only a few feet across. The lake also contains many reefs. Because Lake Victoria is only 270 feet (82 m) deep, some of the reefs are just below the water's surface.

Some of the lake's important islands are Ukerewe and the Sese Islands. Ukerewe is the largest island in Lake Victoria. It rises 650 feet (198 m) above the lake and has thick forests. It is also home to many native people. The Sese Islands chain is made up of 62 smaller islands. It is in the northwestern corner of the lake.

Papyrus reeds grow in swamps along the lake's shores.

Plants & Animals

*L*ake Victoria is a freshwater lake. This means that its water is not salty, like ocean water. The fresh water and its shore are home to many kinds of plants and animals.

Many plants grow along the water's edge. There are papyrus swamps on the western coast. Papyrus is a reed. Ancient peoples used papyrus to make the world's first paper.

Ambatch trees grow on the edges of open water. They have yellow flowers and grow very fast. Water lilies and water hyacinths grow on the lake's surface. They have green leaves and sometimes grow flowers.

Sitatunga live on the lake's shore. Sitatunga are a kind of African antelope. They often live in the papyrus swamps. Their long hooves allow them to walk on floating swamp plants without sinking.

Many of the birds around Lake Victoria are **unique**. One type is the shoebill stork. It is a large bird with silver feathers. It has a broad bill, and can stand still for hours while hunting fish.

Some of the animals on the lake are dangerous. Snails live in the reeds along the lake. They carry the disease **bilharzia**. Certain kinds of mosquitoes can carry **malaria**.

A shoebill stork

Fish

Lake Victoria has many kinds of fish. A variety of different cichlid species are distinctive to the lake. Many cichlid species are mouth breeders. This means that their eggs hatch inside of their mouths!

Lake Victoria has been home to hundreds of kinds of cichlids such as the *Tilapia*. *Tilapia* are important to peoples such as the Luo. The Luo catch the *Tilapia* in mesh nets. They eat these fish, and sell them in the market, too.

Nile perch are also important fish. Nile perch can weigh between 7 and 13 pounds (3 to 6 kg). Some have been as big as 6 feet (2 m) long and 300 pounds (136 kg).

Nile perch are not native to Lake Victoria. Humans brought these fish from the Nile River. People wanted bigger fish in the lake for fishing. Today, Nile perch are an important part of the fishing industry for the countries around the lake.

People use mesh nets and wooden plank canoes when fishing on Lake Victoria.

People of the Lake

*T*he land around Lake Victoria is home to many different peoples. The lake region has one of Africa's largest populations. Two of the main groups that live on the lake are the Luo and the Ganda.

The Luo people live on Lake Victoria's northeastern shore, in Kenya. The Luo are mainly farmers and fishermen. They grow corn and grains, and raise livestock. They also fish for *Tilapia* from plank canoes on Lake Victoria. Men do most of the fishing. Women gather the fish on the shore.

The Ganda live in Uganda, on the northwestern shore of Lake Victoria. The Ganda are a Bantu **ethnic** group. They are farmers. The women grow bananas, their main food crop. The men grow coffee and cotton. They also raise goats, sheep, chickens, and cattle.

Luo people go to the lake for water.

Port Cities

*L*ake Victoria is an important part of trade and transportation for the towns and cities along its shores. Boats from the lake's port cities transport people and goods on Lake Victoria. Some important port cities are Kisumu, Mwanza, and Entebbe.

Kisumu is Kenya's most important port city. It is on the northeastern shore of the lake, on Karvirondo Gulf. It produces sugar, frozen fish, textiles, beer, and ethanol. Lake Victoria and its wildlife are a part of Kisumu's tourist industry. People use passenger boats to travel to other parts of the lake.

The port city of Mwanza is on the southern shore of the lake. It is the second-largest city in Tanzania. Some of Mwanza's industries are meatpacking and fishing. Factories produce textiles and soap. There is also a place for research on tropical diseases. The lake is important in trade with Kenya and Uganda.

Entebbe is in Uganda, on the northwestern shore of Lake Victoria. It has no industry. But Entebbe is important to trade in eastern Africa. Its airport and the seaport connect Uganda with Kenya and Tanzania.

Passenger boats travel between Lake Victoria's port cities.

A Dying Lake

*L*ake Victoria was once known for its various plants and animals. Today, many of these plants and animals are **endangered**. Some are already extinct.

The human population near Lake Victoria is growing. People have cut down many of the trees along the shore. Overfishing has caused some fish species to disappear.

Pollution from cities has upset the **ecosystem**. Industries create waste that gets into the water. Fertilizer from farms washes into the lake when it rains. These things poison the plants and animals.

Animals and plants not native to Lake Victoria upset its natural ecology. Nile perch feed on the smaller fish native to the lake. They eat so much that hundreds of cichlid species are already extinct.

Another species that is not native to Lake Victoria is water hyacinth. This water plant grows quickly. It makes a kind of carpet on top of the water. This makes it difficult to travel by boat, and clogs up parts of the Owen Falls Dam.

Water hyacinth uses up oxygen in the water. It also blocks light from the sun. Fish and other water plants such as plankton cannot live without oxygen or sunlight.

Water hyacinth grows quickly in large clumps that are difficult to permanently remove from the water.

Saving Lake Victoria

Many different groups are working together to save Lake Victoria. These groups are using information gathered by scientists to save the lake.

Lake Victoria Water Resources is a project created to manage the lake's water resources. Scientists study lake water, rain, and land near the lake. This information will help countries that border the lake to manage their lake resources.

Another group is the Lake Victoria Fisheries Organization. It helps fisheries work together to control overfishing. The organization also controls the use of plants and animals not native to the lake's **ecosystem**.

People in other parts of the world help, too. They are using **hatcheries** to breed cichlids and other fish. This ensures that more species do not become extinct.

Water hyacinth also needs to be controlled. One way is to pull it out by hand. Small amounts of chemicals are also used in certain areas.

Another way to eliminate the water hyacinth is with weevils. Weevils are small beetles that eat certain kinds of plants. Scientists continue to study the lake in order to protect it for the future.

Weevils eat plants such as water hyacinth.

Glossary

bilharzia - a severe disease in Asia, Africa, and South America. Symptoms include blood loss and tissue damage.

ecosystem - a community of organisms and their environment.

endangered - when all of a plant or animal species is in danger of dying out forever.

equator - the invisible line that runs around the widest part of the earth, where it is the same distance to each pole.

erosion - wearing or rubbing away of rock, soil, or land.

ethnic - a way to describe a group of people who have the same race, nationality, or culture.

hatchery - a place for hatching eggs.

inlet - an opening through which a river enters a lake.

malaria - a disease caused by mosquitos in tropical areas.

plateau - a raised area of flat land.

reservoir - a natural or man-made place that stores water.

tributary - a river or stream that flows into a larger stream, river, or a lake.

unique - being the only one of its kind.

How Do You Say That?

Bantu - ban-TOO
cichlid - SIH-klid
Entebbe - EN-teh-buh
hyacinth - HI-uh-sinth
Kisumu - kee-SOO-moo

Luo - luh-WOO
papyrus - puh-PI-ruhs
plateau - plah-TOH
Ukerewe - oo-kai-RAI-wai

Web Sites

Water Hyacinth and Lake Victoria
http://www.timeforkids.com/TFK/magazines/story/
0,6277,53607,00.html
Read about water hyacinth and Lake Victoria on this site from Time Life.

Freshwater Ecosystems
http://mbgnet.mobot.org/fresh
This site contains information on freshwater systems all over the world.
Learn about the water cycle, and aquatic plants and animals.

These sites are subject to change. Go to your favorite
search engine and type in Lake Victoria for more sites.

132776

Index